# 365

## BRAINPOWER

## TIPS

365 Brainpower Tips

Text: Simone Harland
Translation: Beate Gorman
Copy editing: MediText, Stuttgart

Photos: Adobe Image Library (4); creativ collection (4); Corbis Images (1), Digital Vision (2); Digital Stock (2); John Foxx Images (1), MEV (23), PhotoAlto (4); PhotoDisc (18); Project Photos (1); Stockbyte (2); SuperGu (2)

© 2001 DuMont Buchverlag, Köln
(Dumont monte UK, London)

The advice given in this book has been subjected to careful consideration and examination by the author, the editors and the publisher; nevertheless, no guarantee can be given. No liability can be assumed by the author, the editors, the publishers or their agents for personal injury, material damage or financial loss.

ISBN 3-7701-7084-9
Printed in Slovenia

# Contents

# Nutrition

Our brain is a miracle of nature. But to ensure that it remains active and fit to a ripe old age, we must provide it with the right nutrition. Many foodstuffs contain substances that can help the memory perform wonders. However, there are also substances that are better avoided so that you do not damage the nerve cells in your brain and keep your memory at a high level of performance for as long as possible.

# 1

Our nerves absolutely require a sufficient quantity of vitamin $B_2$, also known as riboflavin. If your body does not receive an adequate amount of this vitamin, your ability to concentrate can be impaired and your memory can deteriorate. Therefore to keep your brain top fit you really should make sure that your diet contains sufficient vitamin $B_2$. Suitable foods are chicken, almonds, spinach, brewer's yeast, milk and dairy products.

# 2

Protect your brain from the influences of so-called free radicals. These harmful forms of oxygen that damage the body's cells are created in our body every time we take a breath and are a contributing factor in the deterioration of our memory. So-called anti-oxidants such as vitamins A, C and E or copper, selenium and zinc, which are absorbed together with the food we eat, reverse the damaging effects of the free radicals.

# 3

Large quantities of aluminium in our food are one possible cause of Alzheimer's disease, one of the obvious symptoms of which is severe memory loss. Even though this assumption has not been fully backed up to date, you should make sure that you absorb as little aluminium as possible with your food. The first step is to get rid of all the aluminium pots and cutlery from your kitchen, as especially acidic foods can release aluminium from these. You should also use other forms of cutlery when camping.

4

Although the trace element iron is mainly responsible for the formation of blood cells, if there is a lack of iron in the food you eat this will also cause feelings of listlessness and thus affect your ability to concentrate. Therefore, to keep your memory top fit you must ensure that you take a sufficient amount of iron with your food. The body is well able to utilise the iron contained in meat products; green vegetables and nuts are also rich in iron.

5

Ideally, foods that are rich in iron should not be consumed together with other foods that contain substances such as phytic acid (contained in cereals), oxalic acid (spinach) or tannins (coffee). These substances reduce the rate of absorption of the iron that is so important for our brainpower.

6

Vitamin E provides an effective protection against hardening of the arteries, which contributes to our brain not functioning as well as it should and can. Particularly after the age of 30, everyone should ensure that they take sufficient quantities of vitamin E. Foods that contain large quantities of vitamin E are high-quality cold pressed vegetable oils, nuts and linseed. Make sure when consuming vitamin E that your body also gets some fat (in the case of vegetable oil this is unnecessary), as the body can only absorb vitamin E in combination with fat.

# 7

Alcohol damages the nerve cells; everyone now knows this. Every time a person gets drunk, thousands of nerve cells die off that will never be renewed. So as not to subject your brain to this type of damage, which contributes towards memory loss, alcohol should only be consumed in small measures.

# 8

Your diet should contain more wheat germ, for example as an additive to muesli. Why? It's quite simple really: wheat germ contains large quantities of vitamin $B_6$ (pyridoxine), which is involved in the formation of substances that play a major role in the functioning of our nervous system, for example the so-called happiness hormone serotonin. If your body has a vitamin $B_6$ deficiency, this will lead to an imbalance in the nerve system, and a lack of concentration is often the result. Your brainpower suffers!

**9** Lethargy, lack of concentration, depressive moods, and memory loss: All of these problems can be symptoms of an impaired function of the thyroid gland. One of the main causes of these symptoms is a lack of iodine in one's food. Therefore, eat saltwater fish at least twice a week to ensure that your body gets an adequate quantity of iodine and that your brain continues to operate at full speed.

**10** Saltwater fish contains so-called omega-3 fatty acids. According to the latest scientific findings, these prevent arteriosclerosis. A regular diet of saltwater fish will thus help ensure that our brain gets a sufficient supply of blood and that our brainpower is not impaired.

# 11

If you find it difficult to relax it is quite often the case that your brain is not working as well as it could. The reason for this is that our memory also needs a rest every now and then, so that it can work at full speed again afterwards. Peanuts with their high concentration of the amino acid tryptophane, a protein building block, help relax one's nerves and reduce stress.

Do you like nuts and raisins? Great! Nuts have a high concentration of B group vitamins, which help improve our memory. Especially hazelnuts are rich in B vitamins. Therefore, for your brain's sake, crack a hard nut more often.

12

Do you enjoy wild mushrooms? Do you like offal and serve it often? In the interest of your memory, you should limit your consumption of these types of foodstuff, as they are often highly contaminated with lead. Taken in regular high doses, lead can in fact damage the brain.

Make sure you drink enough! Not alcohol of course, but preferably zero-calorie mineral water or juice mixed with mineral water. Our organism requires around $1^1/_2$ litres (3 pints) of water each day to maintain all of its functions. If we neglect to drink enough, our memory also suffers. The best thing is to prepare all the drinks that you intend to take throughout the day first thing in the morning and keep pouring a glass full every now and then.

# 15

Wholemeal bread, peas, beans, lentils and nuts are just some of the foods that contribute to a top fit memory. Besides numerous vitamins, they also contain a substance called phytic acid that belongs to the group of so-called anti-oxidants. It ensures that our cells (including the nerve cells) are not damaged by the negative effects of the free radicals that enter our body with every breath we take.

Vegetables should make up the lion's
share of a diet that is designed to increase
our brainpower or memory in general.
In their outer layers vegetables contain
so-called polyphenoles, which also act
as anti-oxidants and protect our nerve cells
from damage.

# 17

Thiamine – this is a magic word when it comes to keeping your memory as active as possible by means of a healthy nutrition. Thiamine, which is better known by the name of vitamin $B_1$, is absolutely vital for the performance of our brain, as it is necessary for the formation of the glucose that our brain needs from the simple sugars fructose and galactose. If the body suffers from a thiamine deficiency, memory loss and listlessness will result.

Our thiamine reserves have to be replenished every single day, as our body cannot store this vitamin that is necessary for maintaining our brainpower. Wholemeal products and brewer's yeast are especially rich in thiamine, but meat also contains large quantities of this substance.

18

# 19

Brazil nuts are the ideal countermeasure against lack of concentration and stress. These nuts – which admittedly have high fat and calorie contents – are veritable vitamin and mineral bombs. In particular, various B vitamins, vitamin E and magnesium, potassium and iron make Brazil nuts so interesting for people who want to improve their memory.

## 20

Lecithin, a substance that belongs to the group of fats in the widest sense, is an important component of our brain. Lecithin is thus often described as brain food. In our food, lecithin is mainly found in egg yolks, pulses and carrots along with other root vegetables.

## 21

Sunflower seeds are also rich in lecithin. These also promote brainpower because of their high concentration of B vitamins and vitamin E. Magnesium, which is also a good remedy for stress, is contained in large quantities in sunflower seeds.

# 22

The trace element selenium can also prevent memory loss to a certain extent. It is a component of an endogenous substance that belongs to the group of anti-oxidants and thus prevents cell damage. Fish, meat, cereals and pulses are all rich in selenium.

# 23

Just like selenium, the trace element zinc is also presumed to be an anti-oxidant, which can possibly delay memory loss. Besides this, it also carries out a number of further functions in the body. Good nutritional sources of zinc are meat and fish as well as eggs, milk, dairy products and wholemeal cereals. The body can utilise the zinc that is contained in animal foodstuffs better than that which is present in vegetable products.

Being underweight can have a negative effect on our brain's performance – lack of concentration is often the result, especially if we are more than 20% underweight. If you are one of these people who only feel good when they are very thin, you should perhaps reconsider this for the sake of your brain.

24

# 25

Like underweight, severe overweight can also affect our brainpower. While the surplus kilos on the hips do not have a direct affect on the brain, overweight is one of the causes of arteriosclerosis – a narrowing and hardening of the arteries – so that sooner or later, the brain could possibly suffer from a reduced blood supply. In some circumstances arteriosclerosis can even lead to a stroke.

# Short-term memory

We need our short-term memory when we only have to memorise something for a brief period of time. For example, we have to memorise a telephone number as the person from directory enquiries recites it so that we can jot it down on a piece of paper, or we can solve a puzzle in our head without the use of pencil and paper. Unfortunately our short-term memory quite often lets us down: just think of that key you put down only a few minutes ago – can you remember just where you put it? The following exercises will help get your short-term memory back into top form.

Memorise each of the following number combinations for around seven seconds and then write them down.

| | |
|---|---|
| 542984 | 908764 |
| 9563081 | 8263485 |
| 02135873 | 89760238 |
| 57123694 | 24963327 |

# 27

Memorise each of the following letter combinations for around seven
seconds and then write them down.

| | |
|---|---|
| LBRAPX | HLORBN |
| IVIADPR | KPICVER |
| JNWSTKYM | XYJEZNNQ |
| LLTSCHUS | KLRFCPAB |

# 28

Memorise each of the following symbol combinations for around seven seconds and then write them down.

| | |
|---|---|
| \$*+=&? | _-:))/ |
| %§*-+(\$ | !!§/';? |
| //-#+%" | =.=?!() |
| *-+(=)* | &&%\$§!/ |

# 29

Memorise the following word combinations. Then cover the last two words of each combination and try to complete the combination from your memory.

cow – straw-hat – English Channel

telephone – boy – chocolate

underpants – flowers – chewing gum

meadow – skyscraper – county

wren – rock music – bookshelf

# 30

Did you find it difficult to memorise the word combinations on the previous page? Make up little stories using the words in the combinations – the more abstruse the better. For example: The cow with the straw hat on its head swam the English Channel. Using these mnemonics will help you memorise the combinations much better.

# 31

And now once more the same thing with the word combinations. But this time take heed of tip number 30:

rain – hatbox – pope

computer screen – worm – clown

puzzle – artist – window cleaner

island – nutshell – chimney

scientist – pocket calculator – kaleidoscope

# 32

Now, again using the technique from tip number 30, try to memorise the following combinations of four words. Each time cover the last three words and repeat the combinations from your memory.

Morse code – guide – pig – desk

actor – scissors – orchid – catastrophe

coat – aerial – lamp – motorway

**33**

You can memorise numbers (such as telephone numbers) much better if you make up a little story. For instance, you could memorise the number 99 702 in this way: Nena sang "99 balloons ...", Snow White had seven dwarfs, ... love is a zero in tennis, ... and two people belong together.

Now think up little stories for the following numbers and memorise them in this way:

| | |
|---|---|
| 74 19 69 | 98 75 24 |
| 22 26 58 | 36 02 08 |
| 56 38 95 | 91 65 54 |

**34**

# 35

Repeat the exercise from tip 33, this time
with longer number combinations:

| | |
|---|---|
| 87 54 25 63 | 87 54 26 65 |
| 11 22 44 52 | 47 81 16 59 |
| 28 65 41 24 | 75 24 96 35 |
| 00 39 68 87 | 31 59 11 21 |

# 36

Are you familiar with the following situation? You have parked your car in the underground car park and are just about to go out into the street when you start to wonder if you have remembered to switch off the headlights. Situations such as this are common occurrences. Therefore, make it a habit when you leave your car to imagine the car with large, yellow blinking lights on the roof. This unusual image is guaranteed to make you remember to switch off the lights.

## 37

You should learn to use the technique from tip 36 in all situations where you are worried that you might forget something. The more unusual the image that you associate with the respective situation, the less likely you are to forget.

You will not forget to switch off the
cooker when you leave the house
if, whenever you go out the door, you
imagine water flowing from a pot
all over the switch and turning it off
in this manner.

38

Create images for the following situations, which you should not or do not want to forget:

a) Regularly taking a medicine

b) Congratulating someone on their birthday the next day

c) Making a doctor's appointment

Anna: 25.5.2001, 14:30

39

**40**

Now let us go shopping – without a shopping list, of course. Try to memorise the following terms within two minutes:

| | |
|---|---|
| ham | calendar |
| Camembert | flowers |
| milk | pasta |
| wholemeal bread | mustard |
| newspaper | cottage cheese |

Did you manage to remember everything that you wanted to buy? Here too, it is sensible to make up some absurd story to help you memorise the items. This is often easier to memorise than the items themselves.

**41**

# 42

Here is a story for the shopping list:

You gave your dog ham and
Camembert to eat, but then it drank
up all the milk. The cat ate the
wholemeal bread, read the newspaper
and is now looking at your calendar.
It wore a hat, covered with flowers
and pasta, which were spread with
mustard and cottage cheese.

# 43

And now for another shopping list containing more items. Memorise them with the aid of a little story.

| | | |
|---|---|---|
| bread | chicken breast fillet | salmon |
| carrots | apples | Parmesan |
| yoghurt | cheesecake | dog food |
| toothpicks | rubbish bags | shower gel |
| toothpaste | thread | potato crisps |

# 44

The stories that you think up for your shopping lists should be as unusual as possible, as it is easier to remember strange things than things that we see in our everyday lives. A cat reading a newspaper is much easier to remember than a person reading the same newspaper.

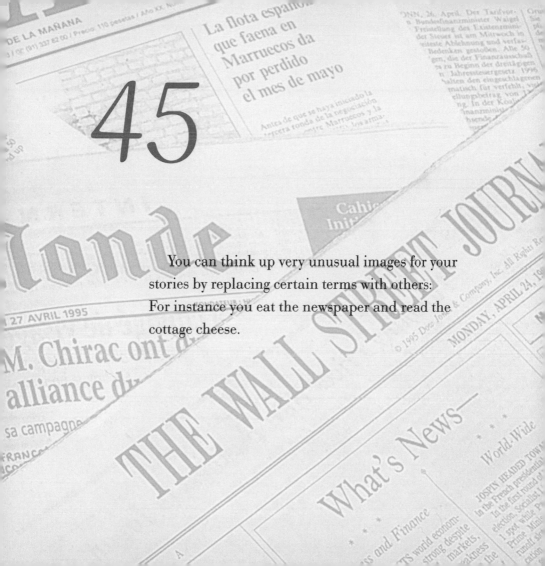

45

You can think up very unusual images for your
stories by replacing certain terms with others:
For instance you eat the newspaper and read the
cottage cheese.

## 46

The more things move in your stories, the better you will remember them. Have the wholemeal bread run up to the cottage cheese and ask for a rendez-vous!

## 47

Exaggeration can also help you to memorise things better. For example, imagine a giant mountain of cottage cheese with an enormous ham rolling down it.

# 48

Imagine the smell, consistency and taste of the things that you want to buy. By combining different senses, you will find it much easier to memorise items. Even if you forget something while out shopping, perhaps you will remember it again when you smell the characteristic aroma.

# 49

Another tip for your shopping list: The more intensively you involve yourself in the story, the more vividly you will see the images in your mind's eye and the easier it will be for you to memorise the list.

After all these tips, here is another shopping list to memorise.
As you know: practice makes perfect.

| | | |
|---|---|---|
| CD | breadcrumbs | peanuts |
| pineapple | tomato paste | cider |
| balloons | wine | shrimps |
| fruit yoghurt | deep-frozen pizza | steaks |
| bread rolls | bananas | zip |

# 51

Now of course there are other methods that you can use to learn your shopping list by heart. However, you have to conjure up the shop where you will be shopping in your mind's eye, then walk along the aisles and picture exactly where everything is that you want to buy.

# 52

A mental walk along the aisles of
the supermarket is especially suitable
for people who can think in images.
Others will find it simpler to memorise
their shopping list with stories.

# 53

But it is quite a simple matter to train yourself to have vivid imaginative faculties. Just try and conjure up the supermarket where you always go shopping in your mind's eye. Imagine yourself walking along the aisles and try to picture everything vividly.

Do you often forget what you have to do the following day? Try to memorise the following list of things to do.

1. Take the dog for a walk before breakfast.
2. Pick up rolls on the way home.
3. Take the children to kindergarten.
4. Take the parcel for Aunt Anne to the post office.
5. Congratulate Uncle Albert on his birthday.

54

Were you able to memorise everything that you had to do? Really it should not have been a problem; after all, it was only five items. But you can memorise things such as these even better if you associate them with a little story.

# 56

Now try to memorise the following things to do:

1. Take the car to the workshop.
2. Go to the hairdressers.
3. Arrange for someone to look after the rabbit.
4. Invite colleagues from work to the garden party.
5. Go to the election for a new works council.
6. Appraise a job applicant.
7. Finish your homepage.

# 57

Particularly things that do not have to be done every day are easily forgotten – the other things have long become just part of your routine. To prevent having to cover your desk (or refrigerator) with little  yellow notes, try especially to fix these tasks in your mind with the aid of outrageous stories.

Now imagine a list of things that you have to do. This list should contain at least ten items, all of which you have to memorise.

58

Extend the list by a further five items and memorise this – admittedly long – list.

59

# 60

Try and memorise the news that you hear on the radio (of course not
word for word, just the headlines). This may not seem to be much
use to you at present, but one thing you can be sure of: you are training
your memory. The best thing is to create an image in your mind's eye
for each headline (for example, oil-covered seabirds for a report about a
tanker accident).

Were you able to memorise most of the news headlines? Then congratulations – you have already trained your short-term memory rather well. If you were not able to memorise all of the headlines, don't take it too much to heart: try again with tomorrow's news.

61

So, now you have trained your memory by memorising numbers, shopping lists, things to do and headlines. Apart from the numbers, there was always a noun present in the things to memorise. Most people find it more difficult to fix verbs in their mind. Try to memorise the following verb combinations within 30 seconds:

eating – climbing – reading

working – telephoning – cutting

sitting – drinking – jumping

inheriting – writing

dancing – falling

measuring – painting

# 63

If you have to memorise verbs, then practise the same technique as for nouns. Simply vividly imagine someone doing these things. An example using a verb combination from tip 62: The boy eats, then goes outside to climb. When he is tired, he goes back into the house to read.

If you can think up other more unusual images, all the better – you will be able to memorise them more easily.

# 64

And now for the same once more, but this time with longer verb combinations. Take three minutes to memorise the following.

1. kissing – playing – sleeping – complaining – cooking – walking
2. seeing – sightseeing – operating – strolling – stroking
3. resting – driving – discovering – falling – dieting
4. exercising – helping – screaming – cycling – repairing
5. whispering – stopping – turning – drying – reflecting

And now, more or less for relaxation,
try to memorise the following combinations
of nouns and verbs within 30 seconds:

kicking a ball – driving a car
getting a fright – making a meal
reading a book – telling a story
stretching your legs – stretching your arms

65

You should also be able to memorise
the following combinations within 30
seconds.

washing dishes – finding Easter eggs
drinking wine – singing songs
ironing clothes – walking dogs
soothing children – planting flowers

66

So, how was it? Have you been successful with these memory techniques? Then try once more with the following terms:

honing a knife – starting a laptop

picking asparagus – cultivating a field

catching fish – peeling shrimps

changing nappies – riding a bicycle

67

# 68

Now memorise the following combinations of adjectives. Adjectives are ideal for transforming into images – so, use the memory technique that you have already tried and tested so many times. Take one minute for the following exercise.

young – crazy – relaxed

small – cute – moody

sweet – cuddly – impatient

shy – elegant – frightened

annoying – strange – nice

pretty – bitter – boring

# 69

Now we have new combinations of adjectives which are shorter, but the list is longer this time. Take two minutes to memorise these combinations.

| | | |
|---|---|---|
| ugly – cheeky | good – cold | robust – strong |
| innocent – mean | bad – big | clever – grey |
| loving – devoted | warm – nice | chunky – sick |
| ambitious – slow | dumb – old | hungry – familiar |

When memorising adjectives, did you try to imagine combinations of the two, such as an ugly, cheeky dog or a good, cold beer? If so, you are well on the way to memorising all of these combinations of adjectives within a very short time without any problem.

70

**71**

Do not give up too easily if the exercises do not work out the first time you attempt them. On some days, our brain is just not as fit as on others.

**72**

If you have problems with the vivid memory technique, remember that you have only been using it for a very short time. At first, it is not so easy to constantly think up interesting images that are easy to memorise, but after some time it will become second nature to memorise things by creating images in your mind.

Now let us make things a little more difficult: The word combinations that you have to memorise this time are made up of randomly selected words – a real challenge for your memory. You have just minute for the first exercise:

below – house – colourful

mosquito – swimming – cold

duck – with – elegant

warm – sugar – crumble

73

# 74

Admittedly, exercise 73 was not easy, but here again the technique of vivid imagination will help you. A few examples for the word combinations: For "below – house – colourful" you could imagine that below your house colourful pipes are buried in the ground; for "mosquito – swimming – cold" you could imagine a mosquito annoying you, and to get away from it you go swimming but the water is cold.

# 75

Here are a few more word combinations of various parts of speech so that you can keep your hand in. Take three minutes to memorise the following combinations:

fish – hunting – without

nephew – green – above

peach – singing – slow

via – arm – young

telephone – discover – behind

fence – bowling – stressed

giggling – in – tent

song – driving – disgusting

ringing – on – carpet

behind – lean – beer

# 76

Memorise the following, longer word combinations within two minutes:

vitamins – depressed – under – atlas – hunger – cake

on – milk – naturally – kitchen – family – flying

elf – dancing – painting – in – artichoke – health

It is much more difficult to memorise a combination of randomly mixed nouns, adjectives and verbs than a shopping list or a list of things to do. If you were able to perform the last exercise without any problem, you no longer need to take a memory aid such as a shopping list the next time you go shopping.

Another technique that will help you memorise certain things is to link them in your mind with something you are familiar with. For instance, imagine your living room and then link the things that you want to remember with items in the room. An example: If you want to buy wine and potato crisps, link the wine with the table and the crisps with the settee. When you are out shopping you then only have to think of your living room.

# 79

You can memorise longer combinations of words (for instance our favourite, the shopping list) by walking through the room in your mind and associating the words that you want to memorise with the items standing or lying around the room one by one. That means that when you enter the living room in your mind's cyc, you should look around the room in one specific direction and keep this direction the whole time you are memorizing the items. If you keep to this rule you will find that you do not get so easily confused.

Now try to memorise the following word combinations by associating them with items in your house:

grass – shoes – milk – chocolate – bread – pliers

sugar – flour – apples – pencils – newspaper – handkerchiefs

duck – cat food – cabbage – gloves – chips

80

# 81

In exercise 80 did you imagine grass growing out of your living room carpet and then rush over to take your shoes away from the radiator so that they do not stink too much? Or did you put milk on the shelf and then quickly take the chocolate from the television before it started to melt? Perhaps you removed the bread from the windowsill and left the pliers hanging in front of the window. Whatever: Images such as this are very easy to memorise for most of us.

# 82

Of course you can also memorise word combinations by associating them with a route that you often take, for instance, the road to work or the route you usually walk your dog. You can often find distinctive signs and objects that you can associate with the things that you want to memorise.

Perhaps you can associate the things that you want to memorise with items on your desk. Of course, to do this, you have to have a good picture of your desk in your mind's eye.

83

84

You can also associate the things that you want to memorise with details from your favourite picture or with items of clothing that you are wearing at the time. The last variant makes things easier for you; after all, you can actually see the items of clothing.

# 85

Now try again to memorise the following word combinations by associating them with other things in your memory. Allow yourself a total of three minutes.

1. dress – dancing bear – seat belt – tea – algae – strawberries
2. envelopes – scissors – orange juice – cucumbers – yoghurt
3. notebook – toothpaste – paper – mouse pad
4. ginger – vanilla sugar – candles – mineral water – nuts

# 86

Using the association technique you should now also be able to memorise the following list, which is slightly longer than the previous lists. Allow yourself two minutes:

diskettes – hammer – magazine – wrapping paper – pizza – wholemeal flour – biscuits – salami – fish salad – piggy bank – cherry cake – wristwatch – pencils

If you could not find something to associate with any of the above examples, then think up some items yourself. It does not have to be your living room that you use to envisage links with things that you have to remember.

87

# 88

The things that are stored in your short-term memory are usually not important enough to be remembered for an extended period. Once they have fulfilled their purpose (for instance, when you have completed your shopping trip), you can forget them again. After all, there is sure to be something new soon that you will need your short-term memory for.

# 89

It is a lot easier to memorise series of numbers when you link the numbers from 0 to 9 with specific terms. For instance, you could link 0 with a circle, after all, that is what it looks like. 1, that's me (= one person), 2 could be linked to gloves (you need two of them), 3 could be a fork (three prongs), you could link number 4 to a compass (four cardinal points) and 5 could stand for your hand with five fingers.

# 90

Number 6 could be linked to a mother (the rounded stomach of an expectant mother), 7 could remind you of the seven deadly sins. A possible link for 8 could be a bee (the shape of a bee resembles the figure eight) and 9 could be a skittle (nine-pin bowling).

91

If you prefer, you can make up your own code for the numbers 0 to 9, as it is always easier to remember your own code than one that has been developed by someone else. Just try it – it is not difficult to memorise a code such as this.

Once you have memorised a code for the numbers 0 to 9 you will have no problem remembering long telephone numbers (or credit card numbers, bank account numbers, bank sorting codes...). This is because when you first memorise the telephone number you immediately associate the individual numbers with the items in your code. The number 98 63 22 is then not just a number; it takes on the meaning of, for example "skittle, bee, mother, fork, glove, glove".

# 93

The word combination "skittle, bee, mother, fork, glove, glove" is easier to remember than the telephone number 98 63 22 – especially once you have converted it into your very own number code.

# 94

Now try to memorise the following number combinations with the aid of a number code. The most sensible thing is to develop your own special code, as this is easier to remember than one that has been "dished up" to you.

| | | |
|---|---|---|
| 52 24 66 98 | 87 52 45 65 | 25 49 63 25 |
| 25 36 89 74 | 25 65 32 65 | 22 57 78 65 |
| 65 76 54 43 | 30 87 47 65 | 11 74 54 36 |
| 21 21 32 89 | 58 58 26 91 | 39 78 82 16 |

In order to imprint your number code in your mind even more firmly, here are some longer numbers to memorise:

980904675121          8493654214          254221474121

654893214584          6591345719          781149654202

95

# 96

If you are in the situation of having to memorise combinations of numbers and letters, allocate a term to every letter in the alphabet that starts with this letter and which·you can vividly imagine. For example A could stand for an apple, B for a banana, C for a cello and so on.

Here are some more particularly vivid images that could stand for the letters of the alphabet:

| | | | |
|---|---|---|---|
| D = dog | E = eagle | F = fly | G = goose |
| H = hyena | I = island | J = jack-in-the-box | K = kayak |
| L = louse | M = mouth | N = nose | O = opera |

98

And here are the last images of this "visual" alphabet:

| | | | |
|---|---|---|---|
| P = pig | Q = quiz | R = reindeer | S = seat |
| T = tiger | U = umbrella | V = violin | W = wart |
| X = xylophone | Y = yak | Z = zebra | |

Of course, the same applies here as to the numbers – it is better if you make up your own images for the individual letters. The reason for this is that if you make your own "visual alphabet" you are much more likely to remember it – the images are more or less conjured up in your mind's eye.

99

# *100*

And now a test to see how well you can memorise number and letter combinations with the aid of your number and letter code. Allow yourself about four minutes for this exercise.

| Z 89 I 99 J 72 | KK 57 NV 49 XQ 73 | 0 ICL 92 LG 41 |
| 65 98 IN MV 8 | PA 50 71 CL MA 32 | 27 21 0 MC JG 2 |
| 32 54 GB DE 5 | BC WD 82 20 NK 2 | 12 0 KS VO 98 H |

# 101

Now that you have had quite a bit of practice in memorising letter-number combinations, you should only require three minutes for the next exercise:

| | | |
|---|---|---|
| O 99 82 JH MP 15 | ZR 35 LQ AP 63 | 95 LC XS 34 21 |
| HG 90 43 88 GH 8 | BY UI 54 29 37 E | OJ AS 85 29 NC |
| SI MB 65 54 TK 58 | GU CH 56 88 LF | NN OI 65 GG CD |

## 102

Do not get overly worried if you do not manage to memorise all the previous combinations in the given time. Take some more time, but be more thorough.

The older you are, the more time you will probably need to perform the exercises – unless, of course, you have already trained your memory by means of other tasks (for example in your work).

## 103

Now we come to another association technique. If you have a list, number the individual items from top to bottom. Associate the number symbol (for example your hand for number 5) with the corresponding term.

*104*

Here is an example of an "association list":

1. (= me): 1 kilogram of carrots
2. (= glove): ice cream
3. (= fork): pickled gherkins

As links that you could associate with your list, you could imagine for instance that you (I) dig up a pound of carrots, pick up ice cream with gloves and eat pickled gherkins with a fork.

# 107

Does this association technique appear too complicated? Do you feel that you have to remember more than before? Just give it a try! When these techniques – in which you should think in terms of vivid images – become second nature, you will find it difficult to imagine how you ever did without them.

## 108

Now attempt to memorise the following list using the association technique described above:

1. Going into the bathroom
2. Changing the baby's nappy
3. Filling in the lottery coupon
4. Paying your tax
5. Buying diskettes
6. Taking a parcel to the post office

## 109

This association technique will also help you to memorise images that are not part of your everyday experience: For instance, change the baby's nappy wearing gloves so that it does not get cold when you touch it.

These symbols for numbers can help you in many different situations. If, for example, you have to learn for a test and have several sub-items to memorise, you can use this technique. Number the items that you want to commit to memory and associate these items with the number symbols.

For example, if you or have to learn something about snails, you could list the following facts:

1. Snails are molluscs.

2. Snails are usually bisexual.

3. Some snails have lungs, while others have gills.

Now memorise the individual items by associating them with the symbols for the numbers. An example: I (the symbol for 1) step on a snail and break its shell.

Now make up your own list of things that you want to memorise. Try to split what it is you have to memorise into concise sub-items and number these from top to bottom. If you have more than nine sub-items, you will have to think up more number symbols for the other numbers, so that you can associate these sub-items with the symbols.

# 113

Of course, you will not be able to order everything that you have to learn into sub-items – many things are just too complex. But still, it is well worth looking for images that illustrate the material to be committed to memory. In this way, you will find that you can also memorise more complicated facts.

# Long-term memory

There are some things that we have to remember over an extended period of time. These include such things as the names and faces of people that we have to deal with again and again. It is, after all, a very unpleasant experience when you have to ask a person's name for the umpteenth time or, worse still, when you address a person by the wrong name. But things and facts that we need in our working lives also have to be transferred to our long-term memory so that we do not have to keep asking the same questions over and over.

# 114

Images do not just help us memorise things for a short period of time – they are also an important means of prompting our long-term memory. Many people are also better able to remember things that are associated with feelings. Therefore, it is helpful when learning to "conjure up" amusing images or pictures that affect our emotions in certain ways.

# 115

If you belong to the group of people that find it easier to remember things when you touch them, in other words, when you literally "grasp" the meaning of the word, you should try to prepare your learning material so that it is not just visible, but also "tangible". In this way you will find that learning becomes much easier than before.

# 116

Some people are better able to memorise things when they hear the learning material. If you are one of these people, you should read out your learning material on to a cassette and listen to it several times. If you do not understand the material yourself, have someone else explain it to you.

## 117

A few people are best able to memorise things when they can associate them with certain smells or tastes. If you belong to this group of people, you could spray specific aromas around the room while you are memorizing so that you can remember the material better at a later date.

## 118

Regardless of which type of learner you are – with the help of images that are either amusing or not a part of your everyday life, you will find that it is easier to memorise your material in the long term.

# 119

Names and the faces associated with them are among the things that many of us find difficult to remember. The first step in memorising names is to pay great attention when absorbing the name of the person you are talking to. If, for instance, the person whose name you wish to remember mumbles or speaks very quietly ask him or her to repeat his or her name – if necessary, several times.

# 120

You will find that you can memorise names easily if
you associate the name with an image. For instance,
if a Mrs. White introduces herself, in your mind's eye you
can imagine her standing in white snow. In the case
of Mr. Green, you could imagine him standing in a green
field or perhaps he has green eyes. If you get to know
a Mrs. Bird, a small or large bird singing its song with a
beak coloured with lipstick could appear before your
mind's eye.

## 121

As a rule, it is relatively easy to make an association in the case of names that have a specific meaning. If you know several people with the same "mnemonic" name, such as Miller, you will have to think up a new image for each of them: For instance, one Miller wears a suit covered in flour, while the other grinds his teeth.

Finding a vivid association for a name
becomes more difficult when the name is not
"mnemonic". In this case you could split
the name into several syllables, each with its own
meaning. As a last resort, you could think of
a rhyme to help you remember a difficult name.

122

# 123

Here are a few examples of how to associate a "difficult" name with an image:

If you meet a Mrs. Ringwood, you could imagine a wood where all the trees have rings hanging from the branches. Perhaps you could remember the name Archerfield by imagining an archer aiming his bow and arrow at a target in a field.

# 124

The best way to remember faces is to look out for especially pronounced features and memorise these. For the one person it could be his nose, which reminds you of an eagle's beak, and for the next, it could be the receding hairline. Even if nothing catches your attention at first, as soon as the person starts speaking or gesticulating, you are sure to find some distinctive feature that distinguishes this person from all the others that you have met.

# 125

Things become rather more difficult when you have to put the name and face together. Now you have to find an image that combines the distinctive external feature with the name of the respective person or the image that you associate with the name.

Here is one example of how to link a face with a name:

You remember Mrs. Blackwood because you saw her serving soup to her family wearing a black dress. Her prominent feature is her light blonde hair. Now you can imagine light blonde hair in your soup.

126

Another example: When thinking of Mr. Softwood, you almost imagine him flying away because of his name. His chubby son also seems so soft that he could fly away.

127

Now pick up a newspaper – preferably a local newspaper. Pick out ten photos containing people whose names are mentioned in the caption. Look at their faces and names, and make an association between the names and faces. Then cover the caption and see if you are able to remember the names that belong to the faces.

128

**129** Two days later, repeat exercise 128 using the same photos. You are not allowed to look at the caption beforehand. Using your visual associations between names and faces, you should now be able to match the names to the respective faces.

After two weeks, take another look at the photos from exercise 128. Do you still remember the people's names?

**130**

# 131

Never, absolutely never, tell someone which associations you use to remember his or her name. The person could feel insulted if they knew that you need a "trick" to remember their name.

There are many things that we have to remember over a long period of time – for example, important appointments are often made weeks or even months in advance. If you do not want to have to write down all your appointments, you should occasionally try associating them with images.

132

# 133

The most practical way to remember appointments is to structure them in the proper sequence. The first appointment is given the number 1, the second number 2 and so on.

The numbers from 1 to 9 (or more) are given symbols, such as those you are already familiar with from short-term memory training. For 1, take the symbol I (= one person), for 2, a glove (two gloves), for 3 a fork (three prongs), for 4 a compass, for 5 a hand, for 6 a mother, for 7 a sin, for 8 a bee and for 9 a skittle.

# 134

Once you have numbered the appointments, associate them with the symbol that corresponds to the respective number. If, for example, under item 2 you have a business lunch with Mr. Cook, your association could look like this: Mr, Cook wears gloves, because on Friday he has to take a very hot meal out of the oven. Now, when you think of gloves, you will immediately associate it with Mr. Cook.

# 135

Memorise the following appointments using the technique described above and call them up from your memory three days later:

1. Computer training on Tuesday.

2. Son Max's football match on Saturday.

3. On Sunday, afternoon tea with Aunt Agatha.

4. Wednesday next week, an appointment with the boss.

# 136

Three days after memorising the list from exercise 135, try to repeat it in the reverse sequence.

# 137

Four days after memorising it, repeat the list from exercise 135 in a random order. You will see that this will cause you no problems whatsoever when you associate the appointments with symbols.

# 138

Now make up your own list of at least ten appointments and memorise it by allocating numbers to the appointments and associating these numbers with the respective symbols. Try to remember this list around a week after committing it to memory. With some practice, you will never again forget an appointment, even if it is not in your organiser.

# 139

By using symbols for numbers, you can also remember the time of the appointment or when the train taking you to an important appointment departs. For instance, if the train departs at 2:34 p.m., think of travelling in a train, wearing a glove holding a fork that is jabbing a compass.

# 140

Perhaps at first you find it rather difficult to make up little stories for the numbers with the aid of images to help you remember things better. But with some practice, you will realise that your fantasy also reaps benefits from the exercise.

**141**

Lines of reasoning can also be memorised easier with the aid of images for the numbers. Try it out next time you take part in a discussion for which you are preparing yourself.

By using these number images, you can easily transfer telephone numbers to your long-term memory.

**142**

# 143

You can also remember the names that are associated with the telephone numbers you have memorised with the help of the number images by using vivid thoughts. For example, to remember Mr. Horsman whose telephone number is 24 33 5, you could imagine a man on a horse, wearing gloves, who is holding a compass and two forks in his hand. Admittedly, this is a rather strange picture, but it is certainly one that you will never forget (especially if you thought it up yourself).

You will also find that you can prepare for important tests much more effectively by using your vivid imaginative faculties. Prepare a sufficiently large notice board containing all the headings of the subjects that you will be required to know in the test. Sub-items are also added to the notice board. Then, while you are sitting the test, you just have to imagine the board.

144

# 145

While you are studying for your test, you should constantly have the notice board from tip 144 in front of you. In your mind, allocate all the information that you absorb to a heading and the corresponding sub-item. In this way, it could be said that you are creating little drawers of knowledge in your mind, which you only have to "open" again to release the knowledge again while sitting your test.

# 146

You should also try to transfer the learning
material itself into images – attempt to visualize
the material as clearly as possible (for example
with the help of the number images), so that you
will find it easier to recall at a later date.

147

While you are studying, your notice board will imprint itself more and more in your mind – whether you want it to or not. During your test you can allocate the questions to the respective heading and sub-item and, in a figurative sense, open up the "drawers" where you have stored the material. Since you have also translated these into images, they will be easier to recall.

Of course, if you have not learned anything, you will not get very far in your test with the notice board alone.

148

## 149

If you find that it helps for your test, instead of a notice board, you could also make up a little book with numbered pages, containing the main headings and sub-items of the learning material. During the test, you can visualise this little book in your mind's eye and will thus be better able to recall your knowledge.

**150**

Before you start working with a notice board to help you with your test, you should train your brain to think in images. Otherwise a notice board will probably not be a great deal of help.

You can train your imaginative faculties each day: Simply take a look at the kitchen table, your desk or any other table containing several objects, for one minute. Then from memory, sketch a picture of the table with the objects on it.

**151**

# 152

The next day, memorise the table and the utensils lying upon it once more. Note all the changes from the previous day and compare your notes with the sketch from the day before. Did you notice all the changes?

# 153

Most of us have the "pleasure" of having to make a speech at some time in our lives – whether it is during a business meeting or at a family celebration. A speech always comes across better if it is made freely, in other words, without reading from notes. You can make a free speech when you associate the most important structural points of with specific items in the room where you will be making your speech.

Take a good look beforehand at the room where you are to make your speech. Also break down your speech into structural points. Now try to associate each of these points with something in the room. For instance, you could associate opening the speech (point 1) with the lectern, structural point 2 could be associated with the left-hand wall of the room, and so on.

*154*

# 155

The points in the room that are to support your speech should ideally be in such a sequence that they are in one direction as you look around the room – in this way you cannot forget any points of your speech. If you should lose the track in the middle of your speech, you only have to concentrate on the following point in the room then you are sure to remember the next structural point.

You can also learn test material in the same way as you memorise speeches. Take a look around the room where the test is to be held beforehand and allocate different segments of knowledge to the different points in the room.

156

During your test, simply let the different points of the room remind you of the material that you have learned. You will find that you are not as nervous when you do not pay too much attention to the examiner.

157

# 158

Learning vocabulary is a horror for most people.

One of the simplest ways to learn a foreign language is to make yourself an index file. It does not matter whether this index is on the computer or if it is in the form of a card index where you write down the words on little cards and arrange these in small boxes – the task of creating the index alone ensures that much of the vocabulary "sticks" in your mind.

# 159

When creating an index file with cards, write the vocabulary that you have to learn on the front of the card (no more than two or three words on each card). On the reverse side of the card write the translations. Make up four or five index files (numbered from one to four or five), but only fill one box with cards.

Now, to learn the vocabulary systematically, work your way through the cards in box 1. When you are able to translate the words on a card, place this card in box 2. So, this box now contains cards containing vocabulary that you have stored in your memory. You do not have to repeat these the next day. However, the following day you have to work your way through the vocabulary from box 1.

*161*

To ensure that the vocabulary on the cards
in box 2 stays in your memory, take a look at the
individual cards again on the third day (you
must run through the vocabulary from box 1
every day). If you are still able to translate
the vocabulary from one card, place this in
box 3. Run through the cards from box 3 once
more after a week.

# 162

And so it continues: The vocabulary from box 1 is practised each day, the words from box 2 every third day, those in box 3 every week, the vocab from box 4, every two weeks and from box 5 every four weeks. When you "cast out" the cards from box 5, you can be sure that the vocabulary on them is well engraved on your memory.

163

Another tip for learning vocabulary: Here too, you
will find it easier if you associate the individual words
with images. For instance, if you have to learn the
word "house" in a foreign language, imagine a house
that you regard as being particularly beautiful when
you read the foreign word. This image will then appear
in your mind's eye every time you hear the foreign word.

If you have a computer, you can consider yourself lucky. And, if you have the necessary cash you can also buy complete programs to assist you in learning vocabulary. There are learning programs available for virtually every imaginable language.

**164**

**165**

Computer learning programs can also help you to learn foreign grammar. Grammatical rules have to be understood before they can be put to proper use.

# 166

If you need some kind of incentive to learn foreign vocabulary, you could arrange the different words according to their areas of application – for example, into words that are required for shopping, words that are used at the workplace, or words that are more suitable for leisure. In this way, the benefit of learning is immediately obvious and the motivation to learn is increased.

# 167

It is also practical to memorise vocabulary in a broader context – this makes the words easier to recall. For instance, if you were to learn the word "family" in a foreign language, you should also learn the words for "mother", "father", "children", "son", "daughter" and so on. The best thing is to write down all such related words on one card and memorise them in this way.

**168**

Everything we have so far said about learning foreign vocabulary also applies to the many foreign words that we are faced with in our own language. Particularly when studying, we have to memorise many new foreign words. It is worth writing these down on cards and learning them by heart.

**169**

Mathematical formulae (for example the binomial formula or Pythagoras' theorem) can also be memorised with the help of index files or computer programs.

*170*

Even information from geography and social studies can be stored on card indexes to help you memorise them more easily. You only have to remember to keep the individual points as concise as possible.

Just before a test, you can run through all the information stored on the card index once more just to make sure. That is much simpler than having to "pore" over numerous books again.

*171*

# 172

In order to memorise sequences of terms, it is useful to take the first letters of these terms and make up new words (of course, the initial letters must remain in the same sequence). This sometimes produces unpronounceable (and difficult to memorise) phonetic combinations such as "MJGZRT"; however these can be filled out with vowels (for example "MAJOGZERT"), so that the whole combination is easier to remember.

# 173

Mnemonics also help us retain things in our memory that would normally be difficult to remember. You know some way of remembering the colours of the rainbow, don't you?

# 174

Rhymes are also useful for helping us remember things. Therefore, if you notice that you have difficulties remembering specific terms, simply make up an amusing rhyme about these terms. In the case of foreign words, the rhyme could even explain the meaning of the word. Admittedly, this all takes a lot of time and effort, but it is worth it in the end – you will not forget the terms so easily in future.

# 175

You will also find that you can remember names much better if you associate them with rhymes. Especially in the case of names that are difficult to pronounce and thus difficult to remember, it is practical to make up a suitable rhyme for the name. Perhaps you can even make the rhyme fit the person?

176

If there are some facts that you are simply unable to remember, you should put them in relation to something that you know a lot about. In other words, store them as additional information to your "special field of knowledge".

# 177

You will find it easier to memorise material that is stored on card indexes if you glue appropriate photos to the index or paint a picture associated with the information on the card. This technique is particularly suitable for people who find it difficult to conjure up images in their mind's eye.

Once you have absorbed the information (when learning, after absorbing the individual facts), you should take a short break, to let the material "sink in". In this way you will find that you are better able to memorise it.

178

You will be able to memorise learning material especially well if you are able to apply the knowledge that you have absorbed. If, for example, you have learned a foreign language, you are more liable to remember the vocabulary and understand the grammar if you have the opportunity of speaking the foreign language.

*180*

A lot of theoretical information simply "cries out" for practical application. If you only learn the theory of how to repair a car, you will never master it as well as someone who tinkers around with cars all day long.

Try to implement the learning material in your actions – even if you only split the material into sub-items and pick out the most important points. In this way, you will find that you can memorise it much better.

*181*

# 182

Talking about the material with others is often more beneficial than cramming for hours on end. You will thus be applying the learning material in the widest sense – you are converting it into actions that are more liable to remain in your memory.

# 183

You can also talk with yourself about the learning
material. It might appear a little strange at first that you
can memorise things better this way, but after you have
tried it once you won't laugh at this suggestion for too long.

# Concentration

The ability to concentrate is closely linked to brainpower – if you can concentrate well, you will be more able to absorb and remember information. Therefore, it is always worthwhile training your concentration abilities. However, do not overdo it at the start – only practice for as long as you are really able to. If you train for too long you will feel as if your head is going round in circles and you will be forced to extend your relaxation breaks.

# 184

The ability to concentrate differs greatly from one person to the next. However, one thing all people have in common is that after long periods of concentration the brain needs a rest. Therefore, always remember to give your brain a break once you have started training.

# 185

In the following exercise, the task is to pick out the letters that are different in each of the following series of letters. Underline them and attempt to solve the task in 30 seconds.

| KJVBB | LJHGN | LCNOP | MASKJ | PLNWQ |
|-------|-------|-------|-------|-------|
| KJIBB | LTHGN | LQNOP | MASMJ | ULNWQ |
| JHGBN | WAXHJ | MLKWE | SWRPU | YRWRT |
| JKGBN | WAXZJ | NLKWE | SWRPI | YRMRT |

# 186

In the following (longer) combinations of letters there is also a discrepancy in each pair of "words". You have 40 seconds to underline the differences.

| JHCMKLJ | BCIKWLJ | ALKJHBC | KDNEIDH | KDNFKEI |
| JKCMKLJ | BCUKWLJ | ALKJHBS | KTNEIDH | KDLFKEI |

| NPRKNBI | GFSCVOP | LBPIEAY | AIUEPOI | YIOLKJH |
| NERKNBI | GFSCXOP | LPPIEAY | AIUUPOI | YIOLLJH |

Here are some more letter combinations
with differences. Take 20 seconds for this
exercise.

**187**

| ZUASDLJ | LKNCLP | SREPJEW |
| ZUAZDLJ | LHNCLP | SREBJEW |

| PKJPLN | NXMLJK | AQWBXYD |
| PNJPLN | NYMLJK | ATWBXYD |

In the previous concentration exercises, the
main concern was to quickly work out where
the discrepancy lay. To do this you do not have
to think too hard, just look carefully.

**188**

Now, in the following series of numbers, underline
the odd numbers. Allow yourself 30 seconds.

89  65  90  76  65  32  12  89  44  99 86  99  54
21  96  32  14  77  31  97  56  41  21  38  92 11
20  10  71  13  54  45  87  74  54  34  68  75  21
21  41  32  65  44  48  74  71  15  28  65  73  80

# 190

Here too, underline all the odd numbers in the series.
Give yourself 30 seconds once more.

784 212 101 369 857 210 321 258 147 652 632
987 523 321 254 586 374 512 120 785 214 987
578 415 783 462 132 233 745 214 258 865 911
874 652 147 475 678 927 531 365 328 695 710

# 191

Once more underline all the
odd numbers in this series of numbers
(Time: 20 seconds).

8754 1452 1257 6547 2147 5465
8798 4512 3269 5415 2478 9874
9654 5458 2874 1478 5447 3695

192

Here is a little tip how to quickly recognise odd numbers: You do not have to look at the entire number, which could be quite long. It is enough to look at the last digit; this is the decisive factor.

In the following series, underline all prime numbers (numbers that can only be divided by themselves and one). You should take 30 seconds for this exercise.

99 71 90 21 32 35 19 12
77 75 64 33 13 98 81 16
93 111 23 96 55 51 3 87
6 88 115 7 65 24 37 94

# 193

# 194

A tip when looking for prime numbers: Apart from the number 2, the numbers have to be odd, since even numbers are always divisible by 2. Therefore, ignore all even numbers – otherwise you are just wasting time.

# 195

Each pair of numbers below differs in one point. Underline the two digits (Time: 20 seconds).

154798 244756 575896 987623
144798 254756 575866 987923

698735 579452 335698 654741
698745 578452 325698 654751

You will often find tasks such as the previous ones in aptitude tests. The idea behind them is to test your ability to concentrate in a stress situation. The more you practise tasks such as this, the better you will be able to solve them quickly and correctly.

In the following string of letters, underline the letters b, p and q (Time: 20 seconds):

pbhgwqpbfgjdbqlonyxqofpk
bjhizxsqkbpiuxlkjhrofhpbhu
lmnbporgfiqzurhpbaysjpbqhj

In the following number series, underline the numbers
2 and 3 (Time: 60 seconds).

5487895421354563259876541256936512547841587 45
2154632145232562365897895425554410230178922 14
6554123212101258745214996366963325875478542125
23214587012303256985623114744147878459832432 24

# 199

In the following series of letters, underline
the letters h and m. Give yourself 40 seconds.

lkjmnhuizknxgdzehkdbnmkllohjiuzhn

opiuzehbcghnmkfjasyxsgfdvxtehdjngm

oiuejdblhjknhcbdgetzthgdbcmkjhguirtg

kjhncheuhenmnbhgyscvdfretwrfdhjebd

# 200

In the following number series, underline the digits 0 and 6. Allow yourself 40 seconds.

65201478451472001236528995421258742145874122548023625
25897541201452865236985421452587411250256221660235689
21478454120112012563699884754785426200214526525421458

You should already have noticed some improvement in your concentration powers. Perhaps you are able to solve the tasks in less than the given time. If not, that is not a problem. Your brain simply needs a little more exercise.

201

# 202

Solve the following arithmetical problems in 40 seconds.

a) $8+3-2$   b) $7-2+3$   c) $2+8-3$   d) $6+7+3$

e) $3 \times 2-6$   f) $4 \times 3+5$   g) $8 \times 2-9$   h) $3 \times 3-5$

i) $21-5+7$   j) $16+8+3$   k) $4+7-4$   l) $3+6+3$

# 203

Solve the following arithmetical problems in 30 seconds.

a) $2+2+2$  b) $9-3+2$  c) $7+4+2$  d) $6-2+3$  e) $5+9+6$

f) $8-2+5$  g) $9-5+2$  h) $3-4+6$  i) $1+4+3$  j) $4-2+9$

# 204

Solve the following arithmetical problems in 30 seconds.

a) $8 \times 2 + 3$    b) $6 + 9 - 3$     c) $9 - 5 + 7$      d) $2 \times 3 \times 2$      e) $8 \times 3 + 5$

f) $6 \times 7 - 5$    g) $9 \times 4 - 2$     h) $(1+6) \times 3$      i) $7 \times 3 - 5$      j) $7 \times 4 + 6$

# 205

Every now and then practice solving little sums that you make up in your head. For example, you could pass the time sitting at the doctor's surgery in this way.

Mentally recite the multiplication tables often. You have probably forgotten one or other of the results – freshen up your (school) knowledge.

# 206

Cross out the word that does not belong to the series.
You have 20 seconds.

a) red, blue, large  b) strong, small, powerful  c) chubby, sweet, fat
d) under, over, and  e) dog, fly, cat  f) amusing, funny, large
g) radio, book, newspaper  h) fish, duck, swan

Solution: a) large b) small c) sweet d) and e) fly f) large
g) radio h) fish

207

# 208

Which word is the odd one out? (Time: 20 seconds)

a) tone, loud, noise, clef  b) book, page, letter, page number

c) carrot, apple, cucumber, cauliflower  d) mouse, snake, squirrel, hare

e) water, fire, air, night  f) in, around, on, are

Solution: a) clef b) page number c) apple d) snake e) night f) are

# 209

In the following exercises you have to form word analogies. You are given a pair of words that are related to one another in a specific manner. For example long–short. Long is the opposite of short. Then, from the following series of words, pick out a term that has the same relationship to the other word.

**210**

Find the analogies to the terms
(Time: 20 seconds).
1) lazy–diligent = fast–?
a) rapid b) slow c) tired
2) hopping–jumping = walking–?
a) running b) driving c) flying
3) dog–barking = telephone–?
a) ringing b) dialling c) calling

Solution: 1b, 2a, 3a

Finding word analogies trains
not only your power of concentration,
but also your feel for language.

**211**

# 212

Find the appropriate word analogies (Time: 30 seconds).

1) book–page = CD–?   a) note b) song c) computer

2) mussel–water = bird–?   a) sky b) air c) fire

3) drake–duck = woman–?   a) man b) dog c) child d) cat

4) car–wheel = computer–?   a) diskette b) hard disk c) internet

5) dread–fear = whisper–?   a) shout b) talk c) dance

# 213

And once more: Find the word analogies (Time: 15 seconds):

1) enormous–tiny = large–?

a) loud b) small c) narrow d) thin

2) head–hair = garden–?

a) plants b) soil c) worms

3) doctor–consulting hours = shop–?

a) opening times b) shopping c) door

# 214

Television quiz shows in which contestants have to pick out the right answer from a selection of possible solutions are becoming increasingly popular. In many cases these questions are very simple to answer; the contestants just have to be able to concentrate. In the following exercises try and pick out the right answer as quickly as possible from the selection of possibilities – the faster, the better.

215

You have ten seconds to answer the following questions:

1) What is the capital of the Czech Republic?

a) Prague b) Bratislava c) Warsaw

2) Which river flows through Glasgow?

a) Thames b) Clyde c) Tees d) Tyne

Solution: 1a, 2b

# 216

Answer the following questions in 20 seconds:

1) What is a sparrow? a) cheeky person b) bird c) piece of jewellery

2) What is a snaffle? a) bridle b) tool c) garden tool

3) What substance is found in coffee? a) cocaine b) arsenic c) caffeine

4) What are algae? a) marine plants b) human genes c) heavy metals

Solution: 1b, 2a, 3c, 4a

# 217

Do you find it difficult to make a decision quickly? Practise as often as you can.

Answer the following questions within 15 seconds:

1) What is a gynaecologist? a) doctor for women's disorders b) fitness studio c) classical scholar

2) What is the capital of France? a) Bordeaux b) Nice c) Paris

3) What is dialysis? a) a special diet b) blood purification c) the dialling noise on a telephone

218

Solution: 1a, 2c, 3b

# 219

Answer the following questions within ten seconds:

1) What is the equator?  a) the Earth's largest degree of latitude b) an exotic drink c) a degree of longitude

2) Which of these is not a nut? a) cashew b) almond c) linseed

Solution: 1a, 2c

Answer the following questions, also in ten seconds:

1) What is chess?  a) a board game b) a card game c) a children's game

2) What is used to make yoghurt? a) cheese b) milk c) pureed fruit

# 220

Solution: 1a, 2b

# 221

Answer the following questions in 20 seconds:

1) In which country is Tripoli?  a) Pakistan b) Libya c) Iraq

2) Which construction on Earth can be seen from the moon?  a) Great Wall of China b) Brandenburg Gate c) Big Ben d) World Trade Center

3) Where is the Red Square?  a) Peking b) Moscow c) North Korea

4) What is curcuma?  a) a type of pumpkin b) a Muslim festival c) a spice

Solution: 1b, 2a, 3b, 4c

# 222

Answer the following questions in 15 seconds:

1) What makes honey?  a) wasps b) bees c) hornets

2) Which fruit contains the most vitamin C?  a) gooseberry b) apple c) lemon d) cherry

3) What was Björn Borg's profession?  a) tennis player b) actor c) rock singer d) football player

Solution: 1b, 2c, 3a

Answer the following questions in 20 seconds:

1) What are measles?  a) a childhood disease b) a tribe
c) a type of animal

2) What is Krakatau?  a) a volcano b) a river c) a channel d) a bird

3) What is Sumo?  a) a fish dish b) Japanese wrestling c) a type of rice

4) What is a taipan?  a) a city in Asia b) a venomous snake
c) a mammal

Solution: 1a, 2a, 3b, 4b

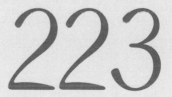

223

# 224

Answer the following questions in 15 seconds:

1) Who played the "Rain Man"? a) Dustin Hoffman b) Cary Grant c) Robert de Niro d) Fred Astaire

2) How long is a marathon race? a) 42.195 km b) 53 km c) 12.5 km d) 40.5 km

3) In which city would you find the Hermitage? a) Paris b) St. Petersburg c) London d) Barcelona

Solution: 1a, 2a, 3b

# 225

Even if you do not know all the answers, you can deduce the correct solution by eliminating the answers that are obviously wrong.

Always decide on an answer quickly. In this way you are training your power of concentration and also your ability to make decisions on the spur of the moment.

# 226

# 227

Answer the following questions within 20 seconds:

1) Which form of government has Canada?  a) parliamentary monarchy b) presidential republic c) parliamentary republic d) sultanate

2) Where were the 2000 summer Olympics held?  a) Canberra b) Atlanta c) Sydney d) Peking

3) Which is the world's smallest republic?  a) Oman b) San Marino c) Liechtenstein d) Philippines

Solution: 1a, 2c, 3b

# 228

Answer the following questions within 20 seconds:

1) What is the famous South African gold coin called?

a) Maple Leaf b) Krugerrand c) Gold Dollar d) Golden Eagle

2) What is the name of former US president Bill Clinton's wife?

a) Hillary b) Sonia c) Ruth d) Madeleine

3) Which of these countries borders Vietnam? a) Philippines

b) Indonesia c) Cambodia d) Turkey

In the following exercises you have to find synonyms – words with the same meaning as the first word in the row. Apart from training your power of concentration, this is also good for your verbal intelligence.

# 230

Take 15 seconds to find the synonyms:

1) stop:  a) finish b) complete c) repeat d) continue

2) friend:  a) neighbour b) mate c) acquaintance d) confidant

3) kind:  a) sweet b) friendly c) charming

Solution: 1a, 2d, 3b.

# 231

Allow yourself 20 seconds to find the synonyms in the following word series:

1) strength:  a) valour b) power c) virtue d) laziness
2) profession:  a) passion b) job c) calling d) work
3) walking:  a) racing b) strolling d) strutting
4) deny:  a) think b) mean c) lie d) deceive

# 232

In the following series of words find the word that has the opposite meaning to the first word (Time: 15 seconds):

1) large:  a) enormous b) small c) gigantic d) powerful
2) running:  a) walking b) moving c) relaxing
3) concentration:  a) restlessness b) peace c) quiet
4) necessary:  a) required b) unnecessary c) important

Solution: 1b, 2c, 3a, 4b

# Relaxation

When we are under stress, our memory often leaves us in the lurch – this is not really surprising; after all, our body has enough other things to do apart from bothering about our capacity to remember things. Unfortunately, when we are in a test situation we are also under stress – and this is a situation where our memory should be at its peak. On the other hand, when we are relaxed, our brain can absorb and retain a lot more and thus allow us to remember important information. This is why it is so important to consciously make the effort to relax – especially in test situations.

# 233

Conscious relaxation does not mean simply lying on the settee and watching television – conscious relaxation means concentrating on your body and spirit.

# 234

If you want to relax, one thing you do not need is to be surrounded by distracting noise. Try to shut out all the noises from the world around you, for example, by closing all the doors and windows in the room. Earplugs can work wonders if all the other measures you have taken to cut out noise are to no avail.

# 235

Noise from outside can be a disturbing factor when you are trying to relax; on the other hand, the sounds of relaxing music or sounds from nature on a CD do not have this effect. A musical background such as this can even be very helpful in enabling you to relax. Next time you are out shopping, look for relaxation CDs.

**236**

In order to get into a state of relaxation, it is helpful to darken the room for a short time and close the curtains to shut out the bright sunlight. In this way you will find that you are not so easily distracted when you want to relax.

Find a cosy place and make yourself comfortable. Stretch out, place a cushion under your head and close your eyes.

**237**

Imagine you are on holiday in the South Seas.
Allow your spirit to escape from the hustle and
bustle of everyday life and send it on a fantastic
journey to a wonderful sun-drenched island.

In your mind, can you hear the waves breaking on the white sand? Do you hear the call of exotic birds and, in your mind's eye, can you see how the palm trees sway in the warm, gentle wind on your South Sea island? Can you feel the warm breeze on your body?

239

# 240

Immerse yourself completely in your wonderful island world. Imagine the azure blue skies, feel the grains of sand under your body and feel how your body is gradually becoming warmer and warmer.

## 241

Stay for some time on your dream island. Only when you feel that you are really relaxed should you slowly open your eyes and gradually return to your day-to-day life.

At the end of your dream journey, your body should feel much lighter, your spirit more alert; in fact you should feel better all over. If a beach in the South Seas is not something that sets your heart alight, you could also put yourself in a forest glade on a summer morning or any other place that you associate with pleasant memories.

242

# 243

If you have problems relaxing the first time you try, do not give up. You are sure to leave your dream destination feeling relaxed the second or third, or perhaps even the tenth time you attempt it. If this is not the case, perhaps you should try some other form of relaxation.

# 244

One other form of relaxation is muscle relaxation according to the Jacobson method. You can learn this from trained instructors or you can also teach yourself. However, if you are attempting to learn it on your own, you should buy a cassette with instructions for the relaxation technique so that you do not forget anything important.

## 245

Sit or lie down in a comfortable position. Take off any constricting clothing. It is best if you wear loose fitting tracksuit pants and a wide top.

## 246

Now clench your left hand to a fist and press your fingers firmly together – hold this position for five seconds. Open your fist and relax your fingers again. Can you feel how good this is?

After ten seconds (switch off your cassette for ten seconds) clench your right hand to a fist and carry out the same exercise once more – tense your muscles for five seconds and then relax them for ten seconds.

247

# 248

Now press your hands against one another in front of your body for five seconds, tensing the muscles in your lower arms. This is followed by a pleasant relaxing pause of ten seconds.

# 249

Now to your upper arms. Bend your arms in front of your body and press your forearms against your upper arms for five seconds; in doing so, tense the muscles in your upper arms. Again enjoy a ten-second relaxation break – your muscles will feel pleasantly warm and supple.

You can also relax your facial muscles. First try relaxing the muscles in your forehead. Wrinkle your brow for five seconds and then relax the forehead muscles. Next, close your eyes and press your eyelids tightly together. After this, relax your eye muscles for ten wonderful seconds ...

250

251

The muscles around your mouth are the next to reap the benefits of relaxation exercises: press your lips together as hard as you can for five seconds. Then relax the muscles for ten seconds. Next, grit your teeth for five seconds and then release the tension. Feel the pleasant sensation that comes over you when you relax your muscles.

252

Now raise your shoulders and tense your muscles for five seconds – again, relax for ten seconds. Draw your arms behind you at an angle and tense your shoulder muscles, hold this position for five seconds and then relax.

# 253

While breathing in, push out your stomach as far as it can go and tense your stomach muscles for five seconds. Then enjoy how your muscles relax again for the next ten seconds.

**254**

To relax your bottom muscles, press your cheeks together for five seconds. As you release the tension, the muscles should feel slightly warmer. Concentrate on this feeling for ten seconds.

**255**

You can relax your thigh muscles by first of all tensing them for five seconds and then releasing them (for ten seconds).

# 256

Finally, raise your toes as far as you can and hold the tension for five seconds. Then release the tension and feel how relaxed your calves are.

# 257

Like the memory exercises, you should carry out these muscle relaxation exercises according to the Jacobson method every day. You only require around ten minutes. But do not regard this as time wasted: afterwards your brain is much more receptive.

# 258

You can learn relaxation exercises with an experienced trainer. Perhaps you would like to do a course in autogenous training, or maybe even meditation.

## 259

Thinking consciously about the nice things in life – especially the little things – also contributes considerably towards helping you to relax (and consequently increasing your brain's receptive powers). Tell yourself that you are going to be delighted about little things in your life at least five times each day.

Go out and experience the pleasures of nature after a rain shower. Appreciate just how good wet grass and flowers can smell and take a deep breath.

## 260

# 261

Go into the forest. Listen to the sounds of the birds and smell the resinous aroma of the fir trees. If it is warm, take off your shoes and walk barefoot on the soft forest floor. But beware of ticks and other biting insects.

# 262

Treat yourself to an aroma lamp and
fill it with an essential oil that is not
too overpowering – preferably an aroma
that induces relaxation. When you
consciously want to relax, light the lamp.

# 263

Go out into the countryside and pick some wildflowers.
Take pleasure in the wonderful colours and the aroma
of the plants. The flowers smell especially intense if you pick
them after a shower of rain.

# 264

On a warm sunny day, find a forest clearing and just sit there in the peace and quiet. Consciously absorb the feeling of sitting on the moist soil with the sun's rays enveloping your body.

265

Sense organic structures.
Take a piece of wood in your
hand, close your eyes and
slowly run your fingers along it.

Stroke a dog or a cat and
feel how relaxing it can be to sense
the creature's warmth and to
appreciate the pleasure the animal
gets from being stroked.

266

Now and again put on underwear made from a material that feels soft to the touch, such as silk. Do you sense how different you feel when you wear this type of material?

267

## 268

Look consciously around you. Try to be as amazed as you were as a child about the little things that you no longer notice as an adult (for example, beetles or butterflies).

## 269

Learn to appreciate again just how colourful and beautiful our world can be. Consciously observe the colours of nature. In this way you are also training your imaginative faculties.

# 270

Find time to go to an art gallery or a museum. Become immersed in the pictures or other exhibits. You will unconsciously absorb many impressions and thus train your memory.

Treat yourself every now and again by turning off the lights in the room that you are in and lighting a candle. Concentrate fully on the light of the candle and the aroma that it exudes as it burns.

271

Listen to a CD with soothing music or relaxing sounds (for instance, birds singing or other natural sounds). Do absolutely nothing else apart from concentrating on these sounds.

272

# 273

Sing to yourself in the bath – it does not matter how out of key it is. You will find that the joy of living that comes over you as you sing will have a relaxing effect and banish all the frustration that has become bottled up inside.

# 274

After a hard day at the office, treat yourself to a hot bath. Lie in the bath, close your eyes and simply let your thoughts wander.

A lovely aroma increases the relaxing effect of a hot bath. But use a bath additive with an aroma that relaxes and makes you dream of nice things.

# 275

# 276

After your bath, massage pleasantly fragrant oil into your skin. Do you sense the stroking movements of your hands? Allow them to slide over your body and take a deep breath to literally "absorb" the aroma of the oil.

# 277

Treat yourself to a regular massage. This relaxes the muscles and thus not just your body, but also your mind. You may find that you are in some pain after the first massage, but if you have a regular massage you will sense just how a feeling of relaxation slowly spreads out to envelop your entire body.

Eat some chocolate (or something else that you
seldom treat yourself to because of your figure).
Let it melt slowly on your tongue, sense the consistency
and consciously enjoy the taste.

278

279

Go for a long walk more regularly. While
you are walking, allow your mind to drift and
try only to think nice thoughts. Put the hustle
and bustle of everyday life behind you.

# 280

Dust off your bicycle and get out and enjoy the feeling of the wind in your hair. Empty your mind of all unpleasant thoughts.

# 281

Put on a CD with some lively music and dance along with it. Try and lose yourself in the movements. Concentrate only on the music and your own body movements.

# 282

Borrow a rowing boat and go for a trip on a nearby lake or river.
The stimulating peace and tranquillity on the water will give you
a completely new perspective on life. Also, the view from the water is
entirely different from the view you get walking along the riverbank.

# 283

Get away from day-to-day stress. When you get home from work, try to
think about other things apart from work. Try never to take grievances
home with you; tell yourself that the rest of the day belongs to you alone.

# 284

Say "No!" more often. If you take too much upon yourself you will not have enough time to relax. The result: Stress will eat away at you; you will find that your memory and power of concentration in general will deteriorate.

# 285

In times of great stress, make time for yourself and take a breather. Close your office door, close your eyes and let your mind drift to somewhere that you find particularly pleasant.

Do not bother about what your colleagues think if you take a rest every now and then. And don't let them disturb you. After your well-earned break, your mind will be free of all the clutter and you are much more receptive for new ideas.

286

287

Homemakers with small children need a short break every now and then. Don't use the time when your child is playing alone to do housework – close your eyes for a few minutes instead and breathe deeply.

# 288

With the help of various breathing techniques you will find that you can relax during the day. Simply sit down and breathe in and out deeply ten times. Pay close attention to the things that are happening in your body as you breathe.

Make sure that the air flows through your chest deep down into your lungs. Now hold your breath for a short time, and then consciously allow the air to flow out, through your chest cavity and out of your mouth.

# 289

# 290

When you are doing your breathing exercises, do not worry if you make loud breathing noises. In this way you can be sure that you really are breathing deeply. Huff and puff as loudly as you like. It might seem unusual at first, but after some time you won't find it so strange.

Of course, you can also do your breathing exercises in the office. If your colleagues give you strange looks and you feel uncomfortable about this, find a place where you will not be disturbed (perhaps the canteen, or if necessary even the toilet).

291

## 292

Remember – stress is the enemy of your memory. If you are under stress you will find yourself forgetting even the simplest things during a test. If your body is suffering from stress, it virtually switches off the memory or at least blocks many of its functions, because it has to concentrate all of its energy for flight or fight – in other words, for physical and not mental powers.

## 293

Even in a test situation, try and remain calm and avoid stress. For instance, shortly before your test, carry out some muscle relaxation exercises according to the Jacobson method, or some other form of relaxation.

# 294

If you find that you have a mental block during a test, simply close your eyes and take a deep breath. Once you have become used to relaxing in this way, a brief moment of relaxation will help you find a solution to the problem.

## 295

Movement is also a very good way of relaxing. It reduces stress and helps us to become calmer and to recharge our batteries. In other words, exercise frees the mind for new thoughts.

## 296

If you are not used to sport, take your time at first. It is better to gradually increase the intensity and duration of training than to be absolutely exhausted after the first exercise block and have no desire to repeat the exercise.

There are many different types of sport that can be practised by virtually any age group. These include rambling, running (with certain restrictions), cycling, gymnastics and swimming. Before starting training, it is important that you consult your GP.

Perhaps you would like to start some form of sport that is not so run-of-the-mill? Many competitive sports can be practised to a ripe old age – admittedly there are some restrictions, but this should not stop you taking up training.

# 299

If you want to practise sport for relaxation, you should limit yourself to training for 15 minutes three times a week at first. You can then gradually increase this to three times 30 minutes, and once you have reached a certain stage, you can even increase this to 60 or 90 minutes three times a week.

## 300

Sport does not just help you relax and thus improve your brain faculties, it also helps keep your whole body healthy. Your general level of performance will improve if you exercise regularly.

## 301

In everything you do, try and do it with your full concentration. In this way, you will improve your powers of concentration as well as find that you are able to perform all your tasks much faster and usually better and more thoroughly than before.

Concentrate even when carrying out menial tasks. For instance, when you are cleaning your house, tell yourself that you are going to do it faster than usual. Save time in routine tasks by always planning to finish them more quickly than you are used to.

302

303

You can improve your powers of concentration –and thus also your brainpower – by concentrating on something in your everyday life for just one minute each day, for example on your heartbeat. As strange as it may sound, you are then relaxing and, at the same time, freeing your mind of all the ballast that has collected.

**304**

By the way, conscious relaxation does not mean simply lying back on the settee, switching on the television and nibbling potato crisps. Conscious relaxation also requires a certain degree of concentration.

**305**

There is no one guaranteed way of relaxing. Everyone must find out for himself or herself the best way to calm body and mind. Many people can best relax when they train hard, while others prefer more tranquil methods.

# Motivation

Have you ever noticed just how indolent people basically are? In order to train your brainpower you therefore may need certain stimuli at regular intervals. In other words, you should motivate yourself to carry out a simple memory training exercise every day. But the same is true in many other areas of our daily lives; without some form of motivation we have no guarantee of lasting success.

The best motivation to increase the performance of your memory is one that allows you to train it over an extended period. Create your own inducement – something that will encourage you to work at improving your memory every day.

**306**

**307**

Small rewards (for example a piece of chocolate that you would otherwise deny yourself) may be a short-term encouragement for memory training; however, they do not provide long-term motivation. Ideal values give us more encouragement to work on improving our memory every single day.

# 308

One type of motivation for memory training is competitive thinking ("I want to be better than my colleague XY"). In the long term, however, thoughts such as this lose their stimulating effect.

# 309

One major stimulus for memory training to encourage you to stick to it could be, for example, the thought of wanting to retain your mental faculties to a ripe old age.

## 310

However, in between times you need small inducements to encourage you to continue "torturing" yourself with concentration and memory exercises.

## 311

There are many small inducements that will encourage you to carry out your daily memory training: perhaps you want to make a speech without reading from notes; or you may be hoping for promotion and want to improve your performance to give you that extra advantage.

Even people who are not currently working will be able to find many opportunities of motivating themselves to continue with their memory training. Perhaps you want to brush up your knowledge of a foreign language and always had difficulties learning vocabulary, or you want to stand out in discussions through your excellent knowledge of a specific topic.

312

Never tell yourself that you cannot do something. Instead, consider how you can best reach your goal. For instance, one can learn (almost) anything if only the right method is applied.

313

314

After each success, take a breather and write down the things that you believe helped you towards this achievement. Perhaps you can effectively apply this success strategy to other areas.

## 315

Do not let little setbacks put you off track.
Remember your previous successes – and
learn from the mistakes that you made
this time. If possible, ask others what they
would have done better.

## 316

If you are nervous about some specific task in your life, take a deep
breath and relax. Then consider how other people have successfully
mastered similar tasks.

# 317

Believe in yourself and in your abilities.
Do not constantly measure yourself against
others. There will always be someone
who can do something better than you
can. That does not mean that you perform
your tasks badly.

**318**

Get used to standing tall. If you always carry your head high, this will have a positive effect on your mental state. In addition, you make a better impression on others.

**319**

If you are not feeling so good about yourself, think positive thoughts. For example, think back to some pleasant experience; allow your mind to float at will.

## 320

Laugh at yourself now and again. This will help you gain a little healthy distance from yourself and the same recurring thoughts that you have and allow you to see things from a different perspective.

## 321

Think about the areas in life where you are really good and about those where you would like to improve. What would you like to do better? And what is the best way to achieve this?

Never set yourself unrealistic goals; instead, consider how you can achieve your objectives step by step. In relation to your memory performance, for example, this means that you should not immediately plan to recite long poems tomorrow, but instead try and go shopping in the supermarket without a shopping list.

322

Draw up a time schedule, stating which goals you want to achieve by what time, and work to this plan. Try and stick to your schedule as well as you can. But do not become a slave to your plan. Some small setbacks are inevitable.

323

324

Really believe that you will achieve all of your goals. If you have doubts right from the outset that you will improve your memory, you will soon loose the desire to train. Write down all your successes – even if they seem trivial to you to at first.

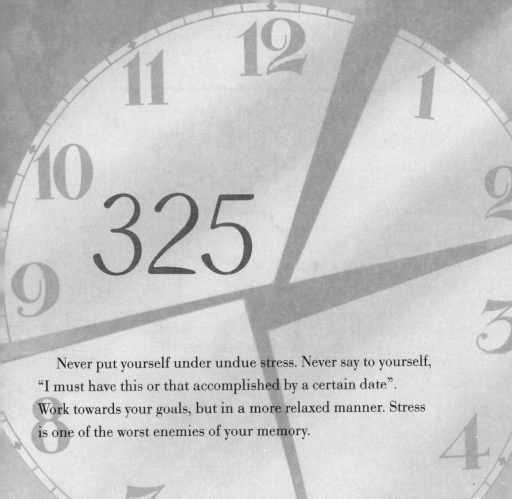

325

Never put yourself under undue stress. Never say to yourself, "I must have this or that accomplished by a certain date". Work towards your goals, but in a more relaxed manner. Stress is one of the worst enemies of your memory.

# 326

Do not tell anyone about your memory training. They could put you under pressure – or in the worst-case scenario, they could make you lose your belief in yourself, by doubting your abilities.

# 327

Remember – no one, absolutely no one has a perfect memory. Everyone forgets something every now and then. Admit this to yourself.

Do not compare your performance with that of others, instead only with your own previous performance. In this way, you will see the constant improvements you are making.

328

329

If you really do not feel like training your memory one day, then don't. Instead do something else practical – perhaps something to improve your ability to relax. The next day, you are sure to feel much more motivated and ready to get down to training again.

330

Remember: you can keep your memory top fit by some very simple methods – even if it is only repeating multiplication tables or memorising names and faces or telephone numbers.

331

You will need your memory for many years to come. Surely that is a good enough reason to find some time each day for memory training, isn't it?

**332**

Perhaps you can be encouraged to train your memory when you can impress others with your ability to remember things. Therefore, do not turn down an invitation to speak at a family celebration. If your speech is good, you are certain to be rewarded with applause.

**333**

Never say, "I can't do that". Instead, always think: "Even if I cannot do it yet, I will learn to do it sooner or later".

# Old age

As most people become older their memory deteriorates to a greater or lesser extent. With advancing age, many brain cells die off and the blood supply to the brain is perhaps not as good as it used to be, since the arteries become subject to hardening to an increasing extent. However, scientists have discovered that links between the brain cells, which make a decisive contribution to our memory, can still form in old age. Therefore, no matter how old you are you should still practise a little brain jogging.

# 334

Provide your brain with new little challenges every day, no matter whether this is simply solving a crossword puzzle or any other type of puzzle. In this way you are even guarding against the onset of Alzheimer's disease.

# 335

The older you get, the more important it is that you pay attention to your lifestyle. Try to eliminate habits that are damaging to your brain, such as the consumption of alcohol, and ensure that you provide your body (and your brain) with sufficient quantities of vitamins and minerals.

# 336

At an advanced age, it is especially important that your body is provided with an adequate amount of vitamins E and C. These help prevent the arteries from hardening and thus contribute towards maintaining an uninterrupted flow of blood to your brain.

# 337

Do not succumb to the false belief that you cannot learn anything new in old age. There are many people who only find the time to study at a university once they have reached pension age.

Tackle something that you always wanted to learn – whether it be a new language or a better understanding of computers.

# 338

# 339

Perhaps you want to pass on your experience and abilities to younger people. There are facilities such as the Senior Expert Service that you can contact if you believe that your knowledge could be of use to others, for example in starting a new enterprise. This will help you train your grey cells – and who knows, you may even really enjoy it.

# 340

In many cities there are exchange groups where you can exchange small services (for example knitting lessons) or home-made items for other services (for example house cleaning) or other objects. Perhaps you would like to join a group such as this. It will help keep you and your brain active.

# 341

If you are still physically fit, perhaps you could offer your services to younger families as a "grandma" or "granddad". And while you are looking after the young children, they will automatically learn something from you. This is guaranteed to keep you in good form.

## 342

Even if your eyesight is not what it used to be, that is certainly no reason to stop training your brain. Talking books and all types of courses are available on cassette and CD (for example foreign language courses). These are ideal for brain jogging.

## 343

No matter how old you are, you can still train your graphic imaginative faculties and thus improve your memory. Take another look at the tips in the first section of the book and pick out a few of the exercises that you believe would be most suitable for you.

# 344

When you are using your mind, do not be afraid to get away from the well-trodden paths that you have always taken. Even if you have always done a certain thing in one way, it is quite possible that there is an even better way of doing it.

# 345

When you are doing your memory exercises, take some more than the given time if you need it. There is no need to rush; the main thing is that you are giving your brain tasks to tackle.

## 346

The advantage of old age is that we are no longer as impatient as we used to be. And patience is particularly useful in memory training – when the results do not come quite as fast as we would wish.

## 347

Again, regardless of age, it is a good idea to set yourself minor goals for your memory training. For instance, tell yourself that you are going to memorise five items from a list in one day; the next day you can increase this to seven items.

No matter how interesting television may seem: do not allow yourself to sit in front of it all day long – get out and become active. Television only promotes the grey cells in your brain to a limited extent.

## 348

## 349

However, if quiz shows are on television (for example, "Who wants to be a millionaire?"), you should take the time to watch them and try to answer as many questions as you can. Shows such as this are quite capable of activating your brain cells.

**350**

When a whodunit is on television where the perpetrator is unknown at the start, try and guess who the criminal could be. In this way you are more involved in the plot, even if you are only a viewer.

**351**

If you do not remain active, you can be left behind in life. This old adage also applies to your memory. Always remember – even when you do not feel much like it, tax your brain a little every day. Ten minutes' training each day are sufficient to stop too much "rust" forming.

# 352

Active relaxation is, of course, also important in old age to get your brain back into top form. Perhaps you would like to learn a special relaxation technique. This has a positive side-effect – you quite often get to know really nice people in these courses (which are also provided especially for senior citizens).

## 353

Start keeping a diary. This will help you to structure your thoughts. As they get older, many people at last find the time for such sensible activities even if they appear old-fashioned by today's standards.

## 354

Always try to think positively. In this way you are much more likely to notice the progress you are making in your memory training than if you start off with a pessimistic attitude.

# 355

Try to spend as much time as possible outdoors. A fresh wind blowing through your hair will help get rid of all these cobwebs that have formed in your head. Your whole body will benefit from the time spent in the fresh air.

Do not lock yourself away at home; maintain active contact to the outside world. This will provide you with a variety of stimuli that will help keep your brain active.

**356**

**357**

Do not just spend all your spare time with people your own age; also try and establish contact with younger people. The (generally) different views of the younger generation will give you some food for thought and this is guaranteed to have a positive effect on your memory.

# 358

If you do not get out of your house too often, then maintain contact with others via the telephone. Once you have finished your conversation try and picture the major points of the talk in your mind's eye once more. This is good memory training.

# 359

If you live alone and it is at all possible, you should consider getting a pet. Experiments have shown that older people who have an animal to care for are usually more physically (and thus also mentally) fit than their contemporaries who do not have a pet.

# 360

It does not have to be a dog. A (relatively) independent cat, a guinea pig or a bird are often more suitable pets for older people.

Look for positive examples.
Peter Ustinov, for example, was
still active in his profession
at the age of 80 – a profession,
as you can imagine, that requires
a very good memory.

*361*

# 362

Find other people to play board games or card games with now and again. These require quick reactions and your mental and concentration abilities are put to the test, so that your grey cells have something to do.

# 363

Even if you believe that you have no artistic talent whatsoever – paint a picture! Among other things, this trains your visual imaginative faculties, which are important for ensuring good memory performance.

Do not compare your mental powers with those of younger people. In many cases the younger people would come off better simply because they are younger – at least if they train their memory every now and then.

364

# 365

Do not let it get you down if everything does not work out exactly as you had imagined. Perhaps the goals that you had set yourself were too high, but there could be other inhibiting factors. Look for the reasons.